In its original sense, Christmas is an occasion for Christians to celebrate the birth of their religious leader, whom they consider to be God.

Over time, this Christmas holiday is increasingly celebrated and until now, Christmas has become an international holiday celebrated in many parts of the world.

Christmas is not only an occasion to celebrate the birth of God, but it is also a holiday for every family. Christmas is an opportunity for members and generations to gather, gather together, confide, share about life, work and welcome an upcoming new year.

Besides, Christmas is also a day for the messages of peace to be spread, and also an opportunity for each of us to share with the less fortunate, the homeless, the abandoned, Loneliness, old age or sickness...

So, this book will give you some wonderful ideas to decorate your house for Christmas as a important celebration in the year.

Table of Contents

Introduction   1
How to decorate the house for Christmas   5
Decoration ideas   49
Fun & fast to decorate for christmas   131

How to decorate the house for Christmas

The holiday season is approaching and the atmosphere is exciting. You will decorate your home with cute and shiny decorations for Christmas and ring at the festival. Decorating your home for Christmas doesn't have to be an expensive thing-just a few simple Christmas decorating ideas can save days (and your money) while making your home look beautiful. You can do it.

Parenting is hard, but what about work and family? In such cases, the Christmas spirit is often in the backseat, but this year it doesn't have to be. Weekends are all you need to transform your home into a Christmas wonderland - best of all, these Christmas decorating ideas are what you and your kids take together and make it happen. into a beautiful string. I'll make it an activity.

Wall-Mounted Wooden Christmas Tree

Most of us don't have big cottages or pouches, so it can feel like a lack of space with a traditional Christmas tree. Don't fret-you'd better have a beautiful tree in your existing space! This wooden Christmas tree has a minimalist look and the best part is that it can be used all year round. Buy some wooden shelves at your local hardware store and cut them in a stackable way to make them look like a Christmas tree.

Mount them on the wall of your living room and decorate each shelf with your favorite decorations. Add colorful lights on and around the shelves. Create a festive atmosphere with candle holders and other Christmas-like stuff.

Fairy Lights Wall Art

Buy a long string fairy light and stick it in your child's bedroom as a Christmas tree. That way, your child will get a cool night light and a personalized Christmas tree just for her room!

Personalized Ornaments

Add personality to your Christmas tree by buying handmade or personalized ornaments. This is something your child can engage in as a fun crafting activity for Christmas.

Get red, white and green pomelo and have your child draw in color. Hang these pomelo on the Christmas tree. You can also make your own snowflakes with popsicle sticks, but they don't have to be normal white. Encourage your child to paint in any color they like. Instead of buying bells and stars purchased from the store, children can cut stars and bells from paperboard and decorate them with tinsel or glue.

A quick tip: Make this a mini decoration party with your kids!

'Memories of the Year' Wall

Build a "memories of the year" wall in your home and post pictures of the outings, trips, and fun moments you've captured throughout the year. This way, you will be able to spend a memorable holiday of the year and share gratitude with your loved ones. Kids can also post pictures of Santa, elves, snowmen, or anything else they like. You can create a photo space on your wall by taking a piece of black chart paper, covering most of the surface area of the wall and decorating it with Christmas elements like snowflakes, hollies, bow and garland.

DIY Stars and Snowflakes

Turn your hallway into a wonderland with stars and snowflakes hanging from the ceiling! Simply download the snowflake and star patterns and have your child color or sprinkle them on and decorate with glue.

Then cut the stars and snowflakes with cardboard in the same way and glue them together. Tie the cardboard with rope and hang it from the ceiling! So every night, you and your child simply look up and step into the winter wonderland.

Utilise Your Diwali Decor

Don't waste Diwali decorations. Decorate your balcony with the remaining Diwali lights and decorate your dining area with green and red tealight candles.

Christmas Treats

Without Christmas delicacies like Gingerbread Man and Rum Ball, Christmas wouldn't be complete! Bake your own gingerbread cookies and let your kids decorate with ice and sprinkles of red, green and white. You can also make chocolate chips and cover them with grated coconut. Place it on a red paper plate and use it as the focal point of your Christmas dinner party.

Rudolph the Red-Nosed Reindeer

Don't forget our favorite food: Red-nosed reindeer Rudolph! You can turn it into a fun Christmas decoration and use it as a gift for your child. Glue the two candies or cookie sticks to a thick chocolate bar and add a small red edible ball in the center of the bar. It you have it-your own Rudolph! Give this to your child as a Christmas treat.

As Dr. Seuss said, "Christmas may not come from the store. Maybe Christmas ... maybe ... it makes a little more sense!" Keep in mind that Christmas isn't just about the shiny things that come with it, such as trees and ornaments. It is the spirit and belief you have. The question is not what is under the tree, but who is gathering around the tree.

Forget all the deadlines at work and the assignment of children at school this Christmas. Please enjoy with your family and loved ones. Celebrate as you like. Sometimes it goes out for Christmas dinner, or it's just snuggling under a blanket and watching a Christmas movie with family and best friends. "It's time to give joy- please promise to give as much as you can to those in need this Christmas. Happy Christmas and New Year!

Decorating a house for Christmas is as exciting as opening a present on Christmas morning. Whether you're welcoming guests to a holiday party or wanting to make your home a cozy and festive mood for your family, this article will show you how to decorate and show the spirit of Christmas. Traditional decoration, a sweet touch throughout the house that shines and adds to the look of the house.

Traditional Decorations

Buy or prune a Christmas tree. Many people consider wood the most important Christmas decoration. If you don't do anything else, get the tree! Choose between real wood and artificial wood. Place it in the room where you and your family will open presents together on Christmas Day.

Decorate the tree in your personal style. Here are some festival ideas:

String of light on the tree. Trees illuminated by white and colored lights are a beautiful sight to behold during the Christmas season. Small white lights are very popular, but you can also buy white, blue, red, or multicolored lights and string them on the tree. Starting at the bottom, let the end of the light strip be long enough to reach the nearest outlet. Wrap the light in a spiral around the tree. Push the other end of the string of lights into the tree branch.

Decorate with ornaments. Consider using fabric, buttons, or crystals to create your own decorations and add a personal touch to your tree. You can also buy classic round boring things and ball decorations from the store. Spread the decorations evenly around the tree, being careful not to leave large gaps.

Decorate the tree with some garlands or some popcorn chains.
Add a topper tree. According to tradition, David's star was placed on a tree, and three wise men led him to him when he was born. It can also be placed on a tree with an angel, a snowflake or other festive decorations.

Decorate around the bottom of the tree. You can buy a white cloth to wrap around the base of the tree. Sprinkle with white glitter as if it were snowing. A gift of the place you intend to give to the people under the tree during the Christmas season.

If you feel that the layout and settings of the tree are a bit too much, try giving the task to someone else to help. The party makes decorating the tree faster and more festive.

Hanging socks. Thread store-purchased or handmade socks somewhere in the same room as the fireplace, mantelpiece, or Christmas tree. Hang the socks using a red or green ribbon or rope. Each family needs to take their own breed.

Don't forget the mistletoe. You can find a little fresh mistletoe in the nursery, or even in the garden or even in the neighborhood hardwoods, but you can also buy fake mistletoe and hang it at the front door. Hang from a small hook at the doorway between the rooms. Tie a small red ribbon to the hook to make it look more gorgeous. And, of course, if you find yourself standing together under the mistletoe, encourage people to kiss each other

Hang some lights elsewhere around the house. Hang some lights on the upper border of the wall where the ceiling meets the wall. If possible, spread some lighting around the room attending most Christmas celebrations, if there is enough lighting to do it.

If you have several homes in the Christmas Village, set up a Christmas Village and show it to everyone. These houses symbolize the times and years gone by and represent what Christmas was like.

Place the manger in the Christmas room or near the Christmas tree. You may want to include the baby Jesus before (if you're afraid to lose him in the original box or forget to put him in the crib later), but it's up to you.

Decorate other rooms in your home. Hang extra decorations on Christmas-specific nails and screws with paper clips. Celebrate everything in the house.

If you are sure that your child will not mess with, mess with, or break the Christmas tree, place it in the nursery. Some teenagers and young adults can trust not to break the decoration.

Show your Christmas card when you arrive. To hang the card, use some railings and window stanchions.

A center table and a table (curtain) will be installed to install the Merry Christmas table.

Get Christmas music ready to play in stereo. Get a CD or cassette, or find a station that plays only Christmas music on your computer. Others can be found in different areas of the internet, but here are three of the most popular and reliable to play all your favorite Christmas songs all year round.

A Twist on a Classic

Perhaps timeless classic black and white realizes what isn't possible with most combinations. Simple and elegant. Whatever you decide to decorate with it, it looks sleek and cool.

There's a reason it's called classic, and that's because it fits almost anything. Your home is no exception. If you like the accent that you get everything else from the contrasting black and white combination, choose it. It can be dramatic but simple.

Liven up the standard

Sure, sticking to traditional Christmas colors may sometimes seem a bit bland, but some creative thinking and new ways to do them are magical.

Christmas accessories in candy colors look great by themselves, but they can look even better. If you're feeling crafty you can even personalize them. Decorating them with ribbons makes them even better.

If you prefer how Christmas decorations used to look a while ago, you can go old school and with the little help of colours like peacock blue, give your home that vintage feel.

The less it doesn't have to be bad

Using traditional decorations does not mean that you should not fax. How do you achieve that? We've collected the best ideas that mean more with fewer shows.

Here are some minimalist decorating ideas that promise to inspire the artist inside.

The less items you use, the better. Nothing stands out more than an item with a strong presence.

Christmas lights can be difficult to arrange to your liking. Therefore, it is better to buy a Christmas tree that already has lights.

If you use too many colors, the item will not only look messy, but also lose its aesthetic beauty. Use only a few shades of the selected color. Looks modern and chic.

Save money by using fruits and vegetables as decorations. It looks and smells good and it's delicious!

Recreate the feel of the outside atmosphere inside your own home. The paper snow lake on the window gives your home a Christmas atmosphere, even if it's not yet snowing outside.

Cut the colored paper into an interesting shape, do some work and use it as a decoration. Easy but effective.

You can calm down with just one color of light on a tree, and look incredible when all the other lights are off.

If you don't have enough time, you can use the Christmas cookie cutter as a great decoration to help you make delicious cookies. Use the ribbon to hang it on your favorite object.

A simple pine cone can also be used as a decoration. Place the pinecones in a plate or bowl and place them on your favorite surface. If you don't have enough pinecones, you can use candy.

Sweet for Christmas, literally cookies. Before baking, poke the cookie dough where you want to make room for the ribbon and then hang it over whatever you like. Bake and it's done! A cookie decoration has been made.

The ribbon can be used as a decoration of its own. You can tie them to any bottle or cutlery to give everything in your home a Christmas vibe. The choice of ribbon color is entirely up to you.

You can tie a bow not only for the ribbon, but also for the handles of windows and doors.

Sophisticated and minimalistic

Simple decorations with subdued neutral colors and natural materials are often one of the best ways to decorate. It combines comfort and luxury while looking at timeless elegance. It embodies the spirit of Christmas and creates a friendly and warm atmosphere.

Christmas materials

Decoration does not have to be made of soft materials. The use of metal pieces as a decoration has proven to be a viable option.

The metallic look is perfect for dark interiors that can be emphasized. Gray works best, although gray mixed with some gold and silver is gorgeous, as everything seems to be in harmony.

A Christmas Dinner

Transfer the spirit of Christmas to dinner. Decorating your dining table with Christmas colors and a variety of Christmas accessories will make everyone sitting at the table a wonderful smile. Not only do they enjoy delicious food, they also enjoy the beautiful views of the Christmas table.

Christmas inspiration

We are used to having to decorate the Christmas tree with all kinds of decorations every year. Christmas is a time of year when you receive a gift of holiday, peace and spiritual stillness.

Each of us has a unique style of decorating Christmas trees, but we do not know the meaning and symbolism of Christmas tree decoration. Colorful lights, tinsel, confetti, candies, nuts, lighting installations and candles hanging from tree branches bring us joy and fulfillment. In addition to these, there are several symbols that make home decoration and Christmas trees even more important.

The famous Christmas wreath hanging on the door of the house, ornaments from Europe symbolizes health and luck. The circle symbolizes the eternal love of nature that never fades. It can be decorated with ribbons, gloves, pinecones painted in silver or gold.

The Christmas tree-shaped stars symbolize good luck and the realization of all dreams. The stars have religious significance and are reminiscent of those that appeared in the sky at the time of Jesus' birth.

Mistletoe is the oldest plant that celebrates winter. It is used to decorate the home with healing powers. For some, it symbolizes peace and harmony. Kissing under the mistletoe brings harmony and understanding, and stronger love.

Whether you are crafty or not, this collection will help you find the best design ideas to create the warmest atmosphere in your home for you and your family. Wish everyone Merry Christmas!

How to decorate your home for Christmas

As it is a family celebration, people gather to dine on cloudy nights and spend time together, so the dining table needs to be decorated accordingly. The personalized Christmas decorations decorate the party table and should not lack the two colors blue and red. The interior design of the room can be decorated with Christmas lights for a warmer atmosphere thanks to the low lights.

DECORATION IDEAS

This is the season to decorate your hall (and trees, walls, doors ... you get the pictures). While you may use store-purchased decorations (or even more convenient, order online), some homemade Christmas decorations that Money can't buy are special and attractive. Good example: These thoughtful Christmas craft ideas and projects are very easy, can be enjoyed for hours with the family, and are very easy (a little extra powder to buy and stock up on children's gifts). You can use it).

From easy-to-make Christmas decorations to simple Christmas table decorations to DIY holiday wreaths for displays, we have everything for your tastes and skills. Handmade wool socks, DIY calendars with galvanized sticks, lots of ideas made with vintage shiny bright ornaments, boxwood chair markers are just a few of the ideas. Exciting ideas on this list. Do you have a hot glue gun? please do not worry! Those unfamiliar with crafting will find a suitable (and adorable!) Project to enjoy.

Bring your creativity to the outside when the inside is complete. We have included some do-it-yourself outdoor Christmas decorations that will allow your front pouch to prepare for the holiday season right away. For example, a wreath made of collectable shiny bright ornaments gives the door a vintage feel, and a "snow-covered" pine provides a natural and organic touch. Let's get down to crafting!

Ornament Trees

Shiny, bright and festive, we proudly present these dazzling beauties every year.

How to: Cover the foam cones with decorations (use 12" and 15" cones) and attach with hot glue. Start with the large decorations at the bottom and move up to the smaller decorations. Let's fill the gap with a mini decorative ball. If necessary, wrap the finished wood with vintage tinsel and beaded garlands.

DIY Tobacco Basket Wreath

Rustic cigarette baskets, fresh greens and bright berries tell the tradition. An oversized check bow adds an accent to the fun pattern. Use floral wires to secure the green areas to a clean bunch and add a pinecone accent.

DIY Door Bells

Hang these "bells" made of minivans and molds over the front door or fireplace.

Method: Arrange mini molds and pans to create a bell shape. Glue them together using epoxy. Heat glue the small ornaments to the bottom to form a clip. Glue the ribbon loop on and hang it up. Add green markers if needed.

DIY Mitten Tree

What is the perfect way to use a losing gauntlet? Triangular screen on the wall of a house in a mud bath or other "gathering" area. Fix the pastel tone pompon decoration to the "twig".

Shiny Brite Center

Place the foot terrine on the plate and place decorations on both plates to create a two-tiered table layout.

DIY Jadeite Plates Christmas Tree

Hang the Christmas tree dinner plate on the kitchen wall. -Use adhesive disc hangers. Add discs according to size, if needed. Secure the vintage Silver Demitasse Spoon using wires and small nails.

Shiny Brite Curtain Tiebacks

Simply thread the ribbon through some shiny loops and tie the ribbon around the back of the curtain to instantly add a subtle touch to your curtain.

DIY Candy Cane

Create your own candyland welcome with these wreaths and stolen ideas.

To make a wreath on the left side: Place the candies in a circle so that the hooks all point in the same direction. Attach them together with hot glue (don't worry if the edges aren't aligned as they will hide the edges). There is a round mint in the center of the top, which overlaps slightly and is secured with hot glue. Hang the ribbon through the two candies above.

To create a garland on the top right: Wrap a 12-inch foam garland pattern with a white ribbon. Attach candy bars, mini candies and mint balls with hot glue to cover the scratches. Wrap a ribbon around the top of the wreath and hang it.

To make a stolen item: Attach an oversized candy and a regular sized candy at different heights and hot glue towards the hook. Tie a bow around the stem and stab the green plant.

Kitschy Candlesticks

Decorate your fireplace or holiday table with some of these easy-to-create festive wall lights.

How To: Heat-bonded ornaments of various sizes onto silver or glass wall sconce.

DIY Dried Citrus Christmas Garland

String dried citrus slices onto a clean plaid ribbon and layer on top of a simple green. Paint around windows, stairs, fireplaces, or furniture (shown here, like this buffet).

DIY Chandelier Christmas Decor

Decorate the lighting fixtures and countertops with green vegetables and berries. Here, cypress branches are pushed into a scroll of chandeliers, and magnolia ornaments are surrounded by pillar candles. Tip: Use unscented candles on your dining table.

DIY Vintage Toolbox Centerpiece

Take a gorgeous wooden toolbox (a classic soda bucket also works), fill it with wood and berry cutouts, and tie it with one or two bows to make it an easy-to-find eyeball. In just a few minutes. Celebration tabletop light candles and other holiday accessories.

DIY Staircase Bows

Add an instant upgrade to your store-bought bow (or tie it with a ribbon) by securing a cluster of shiny red ornaments in the center. Secure it to the garland attached to the railing.

Jingle Bell Table Decorations

Not only does this runner look very festive, it also looks like a Christmas celebration. (These "pearls" are actually red jingle bells!)

How to make: Cut holly leaves from dark green and light green paperboard. Indent the leaf veins using a bone clip or a wooden skewer, then trace the indent using a green pencil. Run to the center of the table and place red jingle bells everywhere.

DIY Layered Garland

Made with fresh cedar and vine branches, this layered wreath looks like a carnival and has a pleasant fragrance.

How to: Bundle cedar and fresh grape branches 12 inches long and hold them together with green metal wire. Repeat until it is enough to go around the door frame. Glue the bundle with the green wire in an overlapping pattern. Hang it on the threshold. Use nails and hooks. Add berries and pinecones.

DIY Book Tree

Make your bookshelf gorgeous with colorful "spine" trees. Place palm trees, greens, and other seasonal trinkets between the books.

DIY Life Preserver Wreath

Add a bunch of marine talent to your fireplace. Here, an antique lifeboat decorated with a festive bow is very attractive. Very little elbow grease is required.

DIY Wooden Spools Wreath

A sweet vintage wooden spool wrapped in a variety of threads, twine, ribbons and lick rack cords provides pop colors. They also hint at the crafts and interesting things that are happening just outside the front door.

DIY Card Tree

A classic and new Christmas response to a timely wooden installation. Put down a galvanized bucket to collect outbound gifts, party souvenirs, or other holiday emails.

DIY Candy Cane Trees and Vase

To make a vase: Use hot glue to attach the candy stick to the glass vase. Tie a ribbon in the center. Full of flowers.

To make a tree: Bake three candy bars in a parchment-lined baking tray at 225 °F for 3-6 minutes until supple. Starting from the bottom, quickly wrap the candy around a styrofoam cone, trim as needed, and repeat until completely covered. Red hot glue hot for mint starlight. It is attached to a tree. To make a star-shaped mint toast, lay a piece of parchment on a baking sheet. Grease the inside of the parchment and cookie cutter. Place the cutter on the top plate. Fill a single layer of mint at the bottom and break to fill the gap. Bake at 350 °F, just melted, for 5-6 minutes. Leave it for 5 minutes. Remove the cutter. Hot star glue on the wood.

DIY Citrus Garland

Homemade decorations are always nicer and cuter than store-bought ones. But a homemade wreath? Well, that's the kind of ambition we want to see!

How to: You will need a navel and orange blood, parchment, two cookie sheets, jute or natural yarn, skewers or nails, and a decorative hook.

1. Preheat oven to 250°F.

2. Cut the oranges horizontally into 1/4-inch slices (4 oranges form a 6-foot wreath).

3. Arrange the cookie sheets on the parchment. Pat the orange slices with paper towels to dry and place in a single layer on top of the cookie sheet.

4. Bake for about 3 hours or until dry. (Turn over with the middle mark so the slices dry flat.) Remove from oven.

5. Use a skewer or nail to make two holes in the top of each orange slice.

6. Thread the string through each hole to even out the orange spacing on the garland. Tie both ends with a loop of string and hang onto the hook.

DIY Winter Wonderland Table Decorations

Do you feel the Scandinavian atmosphere? This table in neutral tones is as delicate as its spirit.

To make a star with wood grain: Draw a pentagram on paper. Make a loop at one end of the silver craft wire. String the beads to the string and crimp the rope in each drawing. Thread the loose end of the wire through the loop, crimp and cut.

To make acorns: Keep the lid natural and apply nuts with white kraft paint. Attach the rope loop with hot glue. Hanging from a spray-painted tree branch placed inside a twisted tube.

DIY Ice Skates Wreath

Why can't you outfit your doors with cool green fur-trimmed skates? Soft "snowball" cotton balls and small silver ornaments complete this crisp door decor.

DIY Dried Citrus Wreath

Magnolia leaves and greens combine to create a simple, natural look, with oranges and dried pine cones adding a touch of color and texture. A delicate burlap ribbon wraps the bundle in a lively and discreet ribbon.

DIY Vintage Tart Pan Tree

Round up a classic tart bread collection that measures 2 to 12 inches and stacks from maximum to minimum. Topped with a classic star-shaped baking pan and attractive snow scene accents!

Grapevine Christmas Wreath

This beautiful Christmas wreath from a family hideaway for fashion designers on Lake Tahoe is not yet complete. An oversized vine wreath is paired with some holiday greens and some handmade pine.

DIY Christmas Stockings

Switch from store-bought socks to colorful socks made from fabric and headbands!

DIY Candy Cane Garland and Candles

Sweeten your holiday decorations with these simple and fun DIY projects with mint and candies.

To make a wreath: Put the candy stick back in a heart shape or with hot glue. Tie a red rope around the stick it glued. Loop and hang the red string.

To make a candle: Use hot glue to attach the candy stick to the glass stanchion. Wrap in ribbon and add pepper
Or mini wreaths and plants for decoration.

DIY Wooden Christmas Tree Forest

The wood scale and finish transforms quickly with green and white handcrafted paint. This whimsical DIY Christmas decoration craft is so easy and makes an ideal project for kids

DIY Christmas Table Runner

This colorful table runner has a simple secret. guess what? Well, we'll tell you: it's wrapping paper!

DIY Wooden Advent Calendar

This plush wooden one has a changeable number block that your kids (or you!) will love to spin around as the moon rises.

Christmas Village

Putting this little Christmas village together is not an easy task. You can also customize all the colors. The pastel birdhouse meets the iridescent "snow" in this fun fireplace decoration.

Eucalyptus Garland

This festive eucalyptus wreath is an extremely clean and sophisticated way to give your fireplace a makeover.

Christmas Village Stocking Hangers

This is a very sophisticated DIY and your friends may not think you really made it yourself. A charming handmade Christmas village sits on top of the mantelpiece and "holds" all stockings.

Apple Garland

Decorate the wreath with apples (pinecones and decorations also work), otherwise add pops of color for a simple green. This choice is especially suitable for assembling the classic signs "Michigan Apple".

Salt Dough Ornaments

These handmade decorations will bring you back to Grandma's house. To make your own, mix 4 cups of all-purpose flour, 1 cup of salt and 1/2 cup of warm water in a mixing bowl.

Knead until the dough is firm and smooth. Stretch the dough and cut it into the desired shape (make a hole for hanging with a straw). Bake at 300 °F for about 1 hour until dry. Cool completely.

Sweater Stockings

Christine and Gabe Bridger, who own this cozy home in Michigan, used vintage sweaters to create their own socks. To sew your own, first take an old sweater, trace it along the neckline, then cut it from the inside out and sew it up. The pleats are (always) sewn in the opposite way.) Using scrap, sew into a loop, then add a monogram using metal house characters.

Tomato Cage Tree

Go to your local gardening center and get a tomato cage. Turn it upside down, push the top of the cage into a bucket or other container, and secure the bottom (now the new top) with a sturdy flower string or twine. Give it a glossy decoration and add green to create a lush background with a colorful bow on it.

Mitten Garland

Collect some discreet gloves for this cozy craft. Then use a large needle to pull the thread from the top down to create an attractive wreath.

Shiny Brite Wreath

Use handmade ornaments and vintage items to transform the basic Styrofoam wreath. After wrapping the base in the ribbon, use the green coated pins to attach the gems to the top until the garland is full.

Christmas Card Holder

Turn your holiday wishes collection into a colorful display with this woodcarving project. Bold with bright colors or keep it simple with light and subdued tones.

Honeycomb Christmas Bulbs

With this blogger's simple trick, you can easily shape a honeycomb ball into a playful bulb and hang it around your house.

Sweater Christmas Tree Decorations

Ribbons or transparent fabric cone flowers foam to form a cute little tree to display on the fireplace, fireplace, dining table or anywhere you need to add Christmas magic to your home.

Christmas Lights Wreath

Illuminate your front door with this colorful DIY Christmas wreath made from vintage light bulbs. Heat-glue approximately 65 colorful bulbs in two rows onto a flat 12-inch kraft or cardboard ring.

DIY Christmas Centerpiece

Join the copper pipes together to make a cute Christmas accent. Just add candles for a romantic holiday.

Homemade Christmas Table Decorations

Hang a small boxwood wreath from each chair (or head only) to make a special chair marker.

Mason Jar Christmas Tree

This idea is great for fireplaces and entry boards. Garnish, grate, and add greens to six canned jars of the same size. Assemble the jar into a pyramid shape, then wrap it in a shiny garland and place stars on top. end!

Tartan Stockings

Turn your tattered plaid blanket and scarf into ribbed socks for a new life. You can do the same with old quilts and blankets in Pendleton or Hudson Bay.

Wood Pallet Tree

Draw a tree on the crate for shipping (you can find it cheaply on eBay or hardware stores) and decorate the wooden slats with styrofoam.

Holiday Shakers

This is definitely a valuable Yuletide idea. Nest a toy tunic and a little deer over "drift" and "iodine" to turn a shaker under $ 1 into a little winter wonderland.

Coin Envelope Advent Calendar

Count down to Christmas with a small paper envelope sized to hold all sorts of surprises, including candies, tickets, and small toys. Use a rubber stamp to print the date on the envelope. You can also add Japanese cards, strings and ribbons for decoration. Then secure the envelope to a clean cork board.

Paper Gift Packets

Shine warm wool gloves and other soft items by stacking two sheets of kraft paper and drawing your favorite shape (star, anklet, or other Eurtide symbol) on it. Cut out both layers of paper, then sandwich the gift between the two shapes and sew along the edges using contrasting threads.

Plain Glass Ornament

These hollow spheres provide a reasonable catalyst for creativity. Place a small wood chip in one and a pretty peacock feather in the other (attached with hot glue on top of the trim). Or drop a model fir tree on a snow-covered globe to create a clearer Christmas scene. You can also use tweezers to put the branches inside or use hot glue to glue a small card in place.

DIY Honeycomb Wreath

Wrapping paper, tissues, and mailing tubes have never been so beautiful. To upgrade your product to a more suitable for the front door, use an X-Acto knife to cut each tube into 2 inch long slices.

Then place the bowl (6 inches in diameter) on a flat surface and use this photo as a guide to place a slice of paperboard around the bowl. Heat glue the slices where those sides meet. If necessary, the bell perch jingle is on the inside.

Paint

It's a penny at the flea market. Some of these amateur paintings can create a unique pruning work. Cut the silhouette of a vintage ornament with stiff scissors.

Box Advent Calendar

Use a regular matchbox at a grocery store to count down the number of days until Christmas. Heat glue the top of the empty box to form a row (start with 9 boxes for the base and reduce by 2 until you have one box). Cut the wrapping paper to wrap each section. Secure with hot glue. Then hot glue the pyramidal columns as shown below. Mark boxes 1 to 25 using number stamps (available at craft stores) and place candies and small items.

Pinecone Ornaments

The spray-painted white pine cones really stand out against the background of trees, wreaths and garlands. As a glitter option, sprinkle glitter while the paint is still wet.

Ribbon Card Tree

Protect your fireplace from snowstorms with this "tree". To make it, you will need two wooden pegs. Cut them into 5 segments, starting at 8 inches wide and expanding each by 2 inches. Fold the two tape measures in half, then place the shortest pin about 6 inches away from the crease and the rest about 5 inches apart. Hot glue the dowels so that they are sandwiched between the ends of the ribbon. Use a small clip to hang the dowel with your favorite wishes.

Christmas Ornament Shadow Box

Give your precious ornaments a special place by displaying them in glossy boxes. Line the frame liner with adjustable wrapping paper or fabric, then attach the trim with double-sided adhesive.

Giant Christmas Wreath

Believe it or not, the shape of this oversized wreath is actually a hula wreath wrapped in a rope.

Mini Baking Molds Ornaments

We love this idea for kitchen countertop wood! But these classic cake pans add sweetness to any plant. Simply glue a strip of hot tape to your back and hang it.

Tea Light Snowman Ornaments

This is the perfect crafting option for a children's Christmas party and a "craft lunch" for baking Christmas cookies.

Snow-Covered Pine Cones

These cute pine make a nice eyeball or attach them to a wreath or wreath for a forest splash.

Rustic Wood Candle Holders

Forget about those expensive store-bought candles for these rustic handmade alternatives. Try and group them, or place them on a fireplace or countertop, as shown here.

FUN & FAST TO DECORATE FOR CHRISTMAS

Building a Christmas tree

This is the easiest and fastest way to add that Christmas charm to your home. The most obvious way to bring Christmas to your home is to add a Christmas tree to your home, no matter what kind of tree it is. It can be large, small, silver, gold, paper, or just a small rosemary plant.

Whether it's a classic Douglas or a white tree with colorful lights, it's the best way to prepare your home for the holiday season. Christmas decorations can be handmade like star decorations made from neutral Christmas tree ice cream sticks.

Hanging Christmas wreaths

A Christmas wreath hanging on your doorstep welcomes guests who visit your home during the holiday, but the inside of the wreath is just as beautiful. Add decorations and other Christmas items to make a flashy red and green wreath yourself, or hang a simple pine needle garland with a ribbon to create a holiday atmosphere. Wreaths are a fun and easy way to bring the Spirit of Uletide to your home.

I use wreaths almost everywhere in my home. The great thing is that you can sell garlands in the store or make garlands from natural elements of the garden. You do not have to spend a lot of money to beautify.

Light some candles

The lighting can set the mood for a really warm and cozy winter day. Illuminating a single candle or a group of candles with some holiday decorations can take these Christmas decoration ideas to the next level. Candles look great as the centerpiece of tables, textures and home furniture.

As a bonus, these holiday candles are fragrant and uplifting with great scents such as cinnamon and scones. Use the candles that are already around the house and surround them with some holiday elements to create the perfect centerpiece without spending dimes.

Bring out some holiday throws and pillows

Adding cozy holiday blankets and pillows in yellow, green, red, or other fun holiday colors is a great way to add warmth to your daily home decor. Plaids, Christmas patterns, holiday colours, and even Christmas-themed DIY pillows are a great way to add cozy decoration to your home. Quick Plaid Throw Tip: I bought a cheap plaid fabric from Walmart and used it as a holiday throw, but no one knew the difference.

Wrap gifts early

Add a Christmas gift and place it under the tree to add a touch of thrill to your holiday decorations. There are countless ways to wrap Christmas gifts. You can also wrap a fake box to make it look like a Christmas gift, put it under a tree, or add Christmas textures before wrapping it. It's his real gift.

Add cute ribbons, decorations and even blackboard gift cards for a nice holiday decoration under the tree. Packing Tips: Discount stores sell beautiful brown kraft paper combined with natural elements in the garden. Cheap and luxurious holiday wrapping paper!

Create holiday inspired vignettes

By creating some simple holiday textures throughout your home, you can really set the Christmas spirit up with some elements. For example, some decorations, garlands, some natural elements from the garden, some candles and a small Christmas tree can go a very long way!

Use your imagination to play with some holiday decorations where you had to create some Christmas vignettes in your home with buffet, dresser, media shelf, coffee table and more. Most of these items in our textures have proven they don't have to be expensive to spruce up with the DIY, free or celebration projects found in thrift stores.

Get your dining room ready

You may not be hosting a major Christmas celebration at home this holiday season, but by adding Christmas decorations to your dining room, you and your family will enjoy a luxurious treat for every meal. Can be.

Simply add a centerpiece candle and green, or your favorite holiday centerpiece, and your dining room will instantly cheer you up for Christmas. Remember that you don't have to spend a lot of money to be beautiful. For a simple holiday look, I created some pea candle centers, glass jars, and candles.

Create a Hot Chocolate Bar

Or a celebration bar of any kind. Making a quick and easy hot chocolate or drink bar is a great way to get your home ready for a holiday party in no time.

Again, this doesn't have to cost a lot and you can use things you already have, such as coffee cups, straws, hot chocolate, marshmallows, and other supplies. In minutes, you can turn your holiday and party decorations from plain to glamorous with this adorable hot chocolate bar that everyone talks about.

Printed in Great Britain
by Amazon